Zero to Investing Hero

Zero to Investing Hero

Investing for Beginners

Kyle Trattner

Published by Tablo

Published in 2021 by Tablo Publishing.

Publisher and wholesale enquiries: orders@tablo.io

20 21 22 23 LSC 10 9 8 7 6 5 4 3 2 1

Table of Contents

Introduction

Before we get started, you should know that you've already completed the most important step of this zero-to-hero transformation: You've decided to take control of your money and start investing.

Saving comes pretty easy to most people, but it takes ***guts*** to wave goodbye to your money without any immediate return. In fact, the only reason the average worker invests is because they can't really afford not to.

So let's dive in and take a look at what you've gotten yourself into, shall we?

What you can expect from this book

This is not going to be some dry, boring lecture on how important investing is, *blah, blah, blah* — because we want you to see how cool and important investing really is. Instead, you'll be getting straight talk and real-life examples to walk you through everything you need to know to start investing.

In **Lesson 1**, we'll take a look at **compound interest** and how it's going to help make you rich. We'll also explain why inflation is your worst enemy and why leaving money in the bank may feel safe, but it's actually the worst long-term move you can make.

In **Lesson 2**, we're going to talk dollars — specifically, **how much it costs to invest** and why you need to be extremely careful about how much you're actually paying for your investments. Investing fees are like compound interest's evil twin, and you should know *exactly* what it will cost to have your money in the market.

In **Lesson 3**, we get specific and explain how to build **a personalized plan for your investments**. We'll take into account what you're saving for, how long you want to invest the money and how you're tackling your other goals.

In **Lesson 4**, we'll get into the nitty gritty of how you can **actually achieve the rapid growth we discussed in the compound-interest section**, using everything from individual stocks to ETFs to mutual funds. You'll get a clear breakdown of the pros and cons of each type of investment, including definitions, so you won't have to stop to ask someone, "What is a mutual fund, exactly?"

In **Lesson 5**, we'll go over **four of the best ways for beginners to buy investments** — and yes, there will be robots. You'll learn how to actually get some skin in the game so you can take your investing plan into the real world.

And as a special bonus, we'll show you some extra resources you can use to keep learning, so you can continue on the path from zero to hero to some kind of mythological investing legend.

OK, while you won't finish this book with a finance degree, rest assured you'll have all the information you need to make the right choices about investments — and to make sure no one sells you a 2.5%-management-fee mutual fund. (Yes, that's super high.)

Why did we write this book?

This is the kind of book we all *wish* we had when we got started.

Everyone understands on some level that investing is important, but it's intimidating when the big banks keep putting up walls — and stapling signs to those walls that say, "ABANDON HOPE, ALL YE WHO ENTER HERE."

We hear all the time about people who get up the courage to go into their local branch and tell one of the financial advisers on staff that they want to put some of their hard-earned savings into the market, only to be told, not so politely, that they don't have enough money to invest.

In a world where it's possible to invest with as little as $10, there's no reason anyone should go through that.

So that's why this book exists: We want to arm you with the basics and dispel self-defeating myths like "I don't have enough money to invest," "Investing is too hard" and "I probably have to spend my weekends reading quarterly earnings reports." None of those is true, as you'll learn over the coming lessons.

Prepare to be amazed.

Lesson 1: Compound interest is your friend

In this lesson, we want to introduce you to compound interest, an investor's best friend.

You might already have learned about compound interest in school — if so, please send us the name of that school so we can send our own kids there.

But, back then, the teacher might not have made it clear just how much money this financial sorcery could make you one day. So let us make that clear for you now.

A brief overview

Suppose that, five years ago, you started saving $100 every month. If that money earned zero interest, today you'd be sitting on an even $6,000. Cool.

Now what if you'd gotten a 5% return on your savings via compound interest? You'd have $6,962.30 today. That's almost $1,000 more – almost, in fact, a full year's worth of extra savings at $100 a month.

Fast-forward 30 years. In the zero-interest scenario, you would still, after three full decades, have only the $6,000 you stacked up in years 1 through 5.

But what if the money had been invested, earning 5% compound interest the whole time? You'd have $30,090.66. *Five times more. Very* cool.

The nitty gritty

At this point, you might be thinking, "OK, I understand compound interest makes me more money, but what I want to know is how exactly that happens." (At least, we hope that's what you're thinking, because we're about to explain it.)

Let's look at the first year up close. And to make things simple, we'll assume interest is paid out at the end of every year. When that interest payment came at the end of Year 1, by which point you had saved up $1,200, an extra $60 (that is, 5% of $1,200) was added to your account.

The next year, you received another 5% in interest. But not only did you earn interest on the sum of your contributions — $2,400 by that point — *you earned it on the previous year's interest too.*

So in that second year, instead of getting $120 (5% of $2,400) you got $123 (5% of $2,460). The $3 bonus is compound interest. It's interest earned on interest *previously earned.*

You don't have to do a single gosh-darn thing to earn money this way, other than finding an account that pays compound interest.

And sure: $3 isn't much. But the long-term effect is what's important — it's what turns $6,000 into $30,000 — and the effect gets more powerful as your money continues to grow.

So that even if, in our example, you never contribute another cent to your account after the fifth year, you'll still earn *$348.11* in interest in the sixth year (5% of $6,962.30). Fast-forward 30 years again: You collect $1,432.89. The effect of compound interest almost quadruples over a 30-year span.

The sure-fire way to lose money (that doesn't involve the stock market)

Let's go back to the first scenario we discussed — the one where you don't earn any interest on the $6,000 you spent five years saving up. After 30 years, you still have $6,000.

You might say, "Sure, I didn't make any money, but at least I didn't lose any, either."

Well, yes, but actually no.

Suppose you want to spend all of that $6,000 today on something you like. Let's say you really like a particular model of basic canvas sneakers, which cost $50, and you want to buy a whole bunch of them. With your $6,000, you'd be able to score 120 pairs. A lot of pairs, but that's your business.

Now fast-forward once again to 30 years from now. You've run through four pairs of your sneakers every year, and now you're all out. The good news is they're still making that sneaker model. The bad news is that the price has increased by about 2% every year since 2021. Now each pair costs $90.57 and your $6,000 will get you only 66 of them.

This is thanks to routine inflation, the means by which things get more expensive and the cost of living gets higher.

If compound interest is investors' best friend, inflation is their archrival. Remember that money itself is not the reason you're investing. Money is just money. You're investing because you want what money *buys* — all the best things in life that *aren't* free. And if you're letting your money sit in a bank account that yields little or no interest, you'll be able to afford a lot fewer of those things than you otherwise could.

The fact is, not investing your money for a return is the same as losing it.

What does investing have to do with this?

Over the long term, 4% average market returns are considered the worst-case scenario.

In 2016, when a major consulting firm forecast that the stock market would average 4% returns over the next 30 years, it was like the entire financial world had a massive breakdown, because that was *horrifyingly* low.

Investors and market watchers had become accustomed to better returns. Over the previous 40 years, the stock market had averaged 7% annual returns, *after* inflation. And that included some major crashes, including the 2008 financial crisis.

Some say those days are over. But even if they are, the one thing everyone still agrees on — even the most pessimistic commentators — is that, over the long term, the stock market goes up.

Which means that investing in the market remains your best hope of earning more than a 2% return on your money and thereby staying ahead of inflation. And as we discussed earlier, you definitely want to stay ahead of inflation.

What's up next?

In our next lesson, we'll take a look at compound interest's evil twin: investment fees. (Yes, compound interest has both an archrival and an evil twin. Life's tough.)

Investment fees are really as bad as everyone says they are, and you need to watch out for them.

We're also going to look closely at the notion of "beating the market." You've heard this phrase, surely. "Beating the market" is what many financial advisers claim they're able to do — and what you should pay them to do on your behalf.

So what do they mean, exactly? Can the market be "beat"? Should you pay someone to do it?

Lesson 2: Beware of fees

In the previous lesson, we learned that compound returns are your new best friend.

Well, guess what? Nobody's perfect. Not even the primal force of compounding.

Compounding has an evil twin. Its name is "fees."

Specifically, fees you pay on your investments. Usually, you'll see them expressed as a percentage, like 2.5% or 0.05%. That percentage is taken out of the money you've invested, usually every year.

Fees are commonly referred to as **management expense ratios**, or MERs. When you see that acronym, think "fees." Think of those fees eating your money while you helplessly watch.

Here's why we feel comfortable calling fees *evil*. Recall that the effect of compounding intensifies over time, making your money grow.

The bad news: Compounding applies to fees too.

Fees will eat your money

In the first lesson's example, you were saving $100 a month. We'll keep going with that but now we're going to look at two different scenarios in which investment fees would affect your money.

The low-fee scenario

Let's say that today you start saving $100 a month, every month, and that you plan to keep up those contributions for 35 years. Since you know all about compounding, you're putting that money somewhere it can earn extra money for you, with no extra effort on your part, and it's earning 6% every year.

You've heard that fees are bad, so you picked investments with an average fee of 0.35%. At the end of the 35 years, your diligent savings habits and savvy investing have left you with a grand total of **$124,168.22.**

The high-fee scenario

Suppose you took the exact same approach — saving the same amount for the same amount of time, getting the same returns — but because no one had ever told you about the scourge of high fees, you paid an adviser an annual average of 2%.

At the end of 35 years of diligent saving and investing, you've got an account balance of **$88,386.62.**

A seemingly tiny difference in fees — all of 1.65 percentage points — has cost you a whopping **$35,781.60**. And to think, the number would have been bigger if you had invested more money.

In Lesson 1, we described compound interest as "interest earned on interest *previously earned*." Well, similarly — and nefariously — investing fees apply to what you've previously earned. They take a bit out of all the money you've accrued to date, not just your yearly contributions. That's how they eat your money. That's their evil game.

"But what if I'm paying fees to someone who says they can beat the market?"

In a lot of high-fee environments, like actively managed mutual funds, the person on the other side of the desk — there's always a big desk; also a well-tailored suit and expensive-looking shoes — will say, "Sure, the fees are high, but you're paying for *performance*."

In the world of money-management, "performance" usually means beating the market every year.

First of all: What does that claim mean?

When the person in the nice suit on the other side of the big desk talks about "the stock market" or just "the market," they're talking about the S&P 500.

The S&P 500 is a market index — a list of stocks, basically — that tracks 500 major companies in the U.S. When someone says, "The S&P 500 is up," they're saying the combined stock prices of all 500 of those companies have increased. And when they say, "The market is up," they're saying the same thing.

And, as you'll recall from yesterday's lesson, the S&P 500 has delivered inflation-adjusted returns of about 7% per year, on average, for the past 40 years — and the most pessimistic prediction for the next 30 years is a 4% annual average.

So "to beat the market," your well-dressed financial adviser would need to design a portfolio that gets better returns than that. Is it possible in a given year? Sure. Plenty of investors do it. Plenty of mutual fund managers do it.

But is it possible to predict *who* will do it? Consistently, every year? These questions have been studied, many times over, and it turns out the answer is always a resounding "probably not."

A 2015 *New York Times* investigation by Jeff Sommer titled "How Many Mutual Funds Routinely Rout the Market? Zero" shows past performance failed to indicate which funds would outperform the market.

And *The Guardian* ran a now-infamous stock-picking challenge pitting professional money managers against a cat. Would it surprise you to learn the cat won?

So if someone tells you they deserve high fees because they can beat the market year after year, ask them to recommend a tailor and then get out of there as fast as you can.

What's up next?

In our next lesson, we're going to build you a custom investment plan. To do it, we'll introduce a method that you'll be able to reuse again and again, to make sound investing decisions for yourself and to get what you need out of any conversation with a professional money manager.

Because the most important part of investing — by far — is being prepared.

Lesson 3: Build an investment plan that works for you

In this lesson, we're going to walk through how to build an investment plan that works for *you*. It's not as difficult as it sounds. Believe it or not, you already know everything you need to know.

Making sound, educated decisions about how to invest requires only that you be clear on the basics. Ask yourself some simple questions: Why are you investing? How long are you investing for? How do your investments fit into your overall financial plan?

Having clear answers to these questions will see you through the inevitable rough patches, when the market is struggling and the media is predicting the worst.

So let's go through those questions, one by one, along with a few more that are just as important.

1. What are you investing for?

Are you socking away your money for retirement? To put your children through college? Just general "savings"? Whatever you're planning to use the money for, it's important to know the "why" behind the money you're investing. The answer affects other parts of your financial plan, and can help guide your other decisions.

2. How long will you keep your money invested?

As we've already established, the stock market rises over the long run. But in the short run, there *will* be bumps in the road. The only way to keep your investment plan rolling steadily over the bumps is to invest nothing that you'll need in the short term.

Look back at Question 1 and think about the timeline of your investing goal. If achieving your "why"will take longer than 10 years? Get that money in the market. Less than 10 years? You might want to take a close look at whether or not the market is the best place for it.

3. Do you have other savings to cover your medium-term goals and short-term needs?

This is key to keeping your head together when the market fluctuates.

If the money in your investments is money you might soon need, and the markets happen to freak out right before you plan to withdraw your money? That's a recipe for disaster.

So you need to have a plan to cover medium- and short-term goals with money that *isn't* invested in the stock market. When the market's acting like a poorly constructed rollercoaster at the county fair, you'll be thrilled that your emergency fund or new-couch fund hasn't taken a serious hit as you go to spend it.

And if the answer to this question is, "Nope, no other plans or savings," then building up a separate stash of cash to cover these things will need to be a key part of your investing plan.

4. How much risk can you handle?

The answer to this question depends on two main factors: your timeline and your personality.

If you're investing for the long term — a period of time you can measure in decades — you have the flexibility to dial up your risk a bit, because your investments have so much time to bounce back from any fluctuations.

But if you're looking at a shorter timeline — especially one less than 10 years — it might be worth dialing down the risk.

In either situation, though, you ***need*** to be honest with yourself about what the finance big-shots would call your "risk tolerance." This is where your personality comes in.

If you know that seeing your investments go down will send you into a "Sell! Sell! Sell!" panic, you must accept that you are someone who doesn't do well with risk. That's OK. Dial it down accordingly.

But if you **are** confident in your ability to weather market fluctuations like a champ, you can probably take on a bit more risk — and reap some higher returns in the process.

Let's put it in concrete terms: Imagine your investments going down by 25% the day after you invest. What do you think you would do? The answer — which, again, needs to be 100% honest — will guide you in determining how cool you really are with risk.

5. How much do you want to be involved day-to-day?

Some people were born to pick stocks, and they can read investment books for *days*. They genuinely, truly like spending time managing their investments in a hands-on way, and doing their own (time-consuming) research.

Other people love not having to worry about their investments every single day. They don't want to spend their lunch hours poring over charts and earnings reports. They read every kind of book *except* investment books.

Where are you on this spectrum? Try to come up with the number of minutes you'd really be willing to spend managing your investments every day, week or month. There's no wrong answer, except one that isn't truthful: A laissez-faire approach can work just as well as an obsessive approach.

6. How much will you contribute every month?

Keeping in mind everything that you've figured out so far, come up with a monthly contribution that works for you, your life and your budget. Don't forget that your investing contributions shouldn't compromise your ability to handle short- and medium-term expenses.

Think long-term: How much do you need to save and how long do you have to save it? More than any other factors, your timeline and ultimate goal will determine your monthly contribution number.

If you're saving for retirement? One rule of thumb is to aim for 10% of your *pre-tax* income every month. But if you can't manage that amount without compromising on your shorter-terms goals, you can work up to it. Better to start somewhere and build than to wait for the day when you can do it perfectly.

What's up next?

In our next lesson, we're going to demystify all your investment options. Stocks, bonds, ETFs — the whole lot. We'll give you the definitions and the pros and cons, so that you can walk away knowing all the lingo you'll need to figure out where your money should go.

We're also going to take another run at our old nemesis: the guy who tells you he can "beat the market." Our mission is to save you from shady investment sales techniques *forever*.

Lesson 4: Confront the jargon

So you're now a card-carrying member of the Compound Interest Appreciation Society, right?

And you've sworn an oath to fight inflation and exorbitant investment fees wherever they may lurk, yes?

And you've got a solid investment plan in hand, one that makes sense for your life and goals?

Impressive!

Now it's time to get into the mud.

First, we need to confront investment jargon. You've been hearing this gibberish your entire life — on the news, in TV commercials, in overheard conversations — and you've wondered to yourself, "What does *any* of this mean? And why am I the only person on Earth who doesn't know?"

The function of jargon

"Investing" is a broad term that covers all manner of concepts that are only ever described in frustratingly obscure language.

Why?

Well, because the more complex and "beyond you" the industry can make it seem, the more money it can charge to make sense of it for you.

So let's demystify this. Here are your basic investing options, assuming you're a regular human being and not a hedge fund with a billion dollars.

Quick disclaimer: These are high-level definitions. The point is just to get us all using the same lingo. Yes, entire sections of the bookstore are devoted to the many subtleties and particularities of each of the following categories. Don't worry about it. You're about to learn everything you *need* to know.

Stocks

A stock is a unit of ownership in a company. Literally, if you own a stock, you own a part of the company, and you have a proportionate claim to its assets and earnings.

Pros: If you're buying and holding stocks yourself, you skip over management fees entirely. You're doing yourself what advisers want to charge you to do on your behalf.

Cons: Buying your own stocks and choosing companies to invest in can be a time-consuming and tricky endeavor. A lot of stress comes with trying to pick "winners."

Bonds

A bond is a loan, but in this case *you're* the bank. Bonds can be issued by companies and governments of all sizes, and the whole process is pretty simple. You buy a bond, they get your money, and you get a guaranteed interest payment from them until a specified point in the future, when — this part is good — you get your original money back.

Pros: Bonds are a great way to balance out riskier investments because they guarantee a small but sure-fire rate of return. The only way you lose is if the company or government collapses.

Cons: Because they're low-risk, the interest is generally low. So if all you had were bonds, it would be hard to achieve the return you need to really grow your money.

Mutual funds

A professional (or, more likely, a team of professionals) chooses a combination of stocks, bonds and commodities, usually along a certain theme, and charges you a fee to invest your money in that special mix.

Pros: They can invest you in really specific parts of the market. For example, you say, "I want to buy a fund that tracks the maple syrup industry in Canada." Chances are, there's a fund out there made up only of stocks in Canadian maple syrup companies.

Cons: Usually, this kind of active management — paying professionals to pick stocks and bonds — comes with really high fees. Think 2% or higher. *No good.*

Index funds

An index fund is a collection of stocks that tries to match the performance of a market index by holding the same stocks, in the same proportions, that make up that index.

For example, remember the S&P 500 market index we referenced earlier? An index fund that tries to match it would hold a chunk of all 500 of those companies.

Basically, an index fund is a type of mutual fund with a few key differences: It's trying to match the market, not beat it, and it's usually way cheaper for investors to hold.

Pros: Because they correspond to existing lists of stocks and bonds, there's very little need for active management. That keeps your costs down.

Cons: If you're actually trying to beat the market, or want to pick your own stocks, this isn't the right option for you. Index funds don't offer flexibility or creativity. It's a pre-set package deal.

ETF

An exchange-traded fund (ETF) is bought and sold like a stock but works like an index fund. It can be made up of stocks, bonds and other investments that aim to track the performance of … well, something.

That's a key distinction: ETFs can track the same indexes as index funds, but they can track other things, too.

Pros: Usually, ETFs have even lower fees than index funds: 0.05% is not unheard of. That is the lowest of the low. *Fantastic.*

Cons: ETFs can be tricky to buy. Traditional brokerages sell ETFs, but they do so at a price. You might have to pay high commissions on their trades or steep fees to maintain their brokerage accounts.

The importance of diversifying (and Norse mythology)

Congratulations — you've slain the jargon. Seriously. Almost all the fancy-sounding investing talk you hear in the wild relates in some way to the concepts we just discussed.

And now that we know about the different types of investments, we have to discuss the importance of diversifying those investments.

Let's use college as a model here.

You're studying Norse mythology, which you love. Sure, you got into it because of Thor in the Avengers, but it turns out the whole field agrees with you. Still, though, if all your courses are focused on Norse mythology, you'll be banking on that one specific field for a job after you graduate.

Take it from us: It's hard out there for Norse mythologists these days.

But let's say that you took a few accounting classes on the side, as your electives. Just to diversify your skillset. Now when you graduate, you've got options, thanks to your handy accounting classes.

That's what diversifying is all about: making sure you have more than one way to succeed.

You can see how this principle applies to investing. You want to make sure you diversify the mix of investments you choose. If you have $100,000 to invest, and you put it all into a single stock? Well, what if that stock is the Norse mythology of the investing world? Wouldn't it be great to have some accounting classes to fall back on?

By including different types of investments, with different risk profiles, exposed to different parts of the world and different industries, you're going to be covered if any of them fails spectacularly. And even if that happens, you've given yourself enough time to watch it recover, remember?

What's up next?

In our next lesson, we're going to look at how you can now, actually, put some real skin in the game.

Money, that is. We're talking about money. You're going to invest it, and it's going to be fun.

We'll talk about human advisers, robo-advisers, banks and more. We'll focus on the options available to real people, not hedge-fund billionaires. (If you are a hedge-fund billionaire, *why are you even reading this book?)*

Lesson 5: Take the Big Step

In this lesson, we're going to talk about some of the most accessible ways for you to actually invest your money.

If you're worried you're not ready for this, don't be. Think about everything you've learned these last four lessons.

- You understand the magic of compounding.
- You know that inflation and fees will eat your savings.
- You've honestly assessed what you want to get out of investing and how much time and money you want to put into it.
- You have a solid grasp on the investing terminology you need to know, and you're clear on the importance of diversification.

Make no mistake — you are ready for this.

So let's take the Big Step and get your money invested.

The best beginner-friendly investing options

We've already said that this is not a book for hedge-fund billionaires — we've said it a couple of times, actually — but it bears repeating. Keep that in mind as read through this lesson.

We'll tell you about some of the best options for people who are ready to get started with investing, but understand that there are many more options out there. There are as many different ways to invest as there are different kinds of investors.

But we think these are the best places to start, so here we go.

Robo-advisers

These are online wealth-management services that automate every part of investing, using algorithms and other impressive-sounding technology. They can build you a balanced, low-cost portfolio and handle all the details, and many of them have real-life humans you can talk to if you need to. Generally, they take a passive approach to managing the money you invest with them, so don't expect to hear them tell you how they're going to beat the market for you.

Pros: Really easy to use, from sign-up to ongoing management. It's pretty much a set-it-and-forget-it approach, and takes very little time or effort to "manage."

Cons: If you're not comfortable with technology, you might not like the online-only experience. And the fees they charge are more than you'd pay for a totally DIY approach.

Robo-advisers are probably right for you if ...

You want to keep fees low but you don't feel ready to build your own portfolio all by yourself — and you want to start small. Most robo-advisers have very small minimum investments, and some have no minimums.

Real human financial advisers

These are people who, in exchange for a fee, will guide you on all sorts of financial decisions, including investments. Some financial advisers will manage your investments for you, while others will recommend services that you can use on your own, depending on your level of comfort and experience.

You should always look for an adviser who has, or is working toward, a certified financial planner (CFP) designation, which among other things requires that they act as a fiduciary. *(That's a fancy legal term for an adviser who puts their clients' interests ahead of their own.)*

Pros: You get entirely customized, one-on-one advice, from a real human being — no need to DIY anything. If they're a CFP, they will usually take your whole financial situation into account as well, not just your investments.

Cons: You need to be *really* clear on how much you're paying for advice, since different advisers have different fee structures. Some charge a percentage of your invested assets (they call that AUM for "assets under management") while others just charge a flat fee for building you a plan and giving you advice.

A financial adviser is right for you if ...

You really want one-on-one guidance that's specific to your financial situation, or your financial situation is complex. They're the experts, and if you're working with some complicated money stuff, you can trust a CFP to keep you safe and sound.

Your bank

Your bank's financial advisers can offer advice and set up your investments for you, usually without you needing to do much at all. Generally, they offer a range of mutual funds and similar options.

Pros: Everything is pretty much taken care of for you, and you can get everything set up in the course of a single meeting at the bank. From there, things basically run on autopilot.

Cons: *Fees.* Bank mutual funds are notoriously high-fee investments, many of them clocking in at higher than 2% MER. You pay a whole lot of money for the convenience of investing with your bank. Plus, those advisers you're talking to likely get paid commission or have sales targets tied to high-fee mutual funds. ***That means their interests aren't always aligned with yours.***

Investing with your bank is right for you if ...

You trust your bank's financial adviser to help you figure out a plan that works for you, and you're ready to pay close attention to the fees they're charging — and to ask the hard questions about those fees. Most banks have low-fee options available, so if you go in knowing what you want, it could be a great fit. Your bank will also likely be able to accommodate any portfolio size, but be careful: Some banks charge extra fees to manage small accounts.

Online brokerages

These are services that allow *you,* not an adviser, to build your own portfolio of stocks, ETFs and more — the range of options depends on the brokerage you choose. This is the DIY dream: full control of exactly what you buy and how much.

Pros: We'll say it again: full control. And generally the lowest fee structures around. This approach is how you can buy those 0.05% ETFs.

Cons: Getting set up can be tricky, and after that it's up to you to do everything from choosing investment vehicles to rebalancing your portfolio. Definitely not a hands-off approach.

An online brokerage is right for you if ...

You're ready to get your hands dirty and put in the work to reap those sweet, sweet low fees. You're OK with making all the decisions, and you're confident about things like rebalancing your own portfolio.

***

So there you have it — the best options for the new investor. Again: these are not *all* the investing options available to you. Not by a long shot. But we think these are the places where you should start.

What's up next?

Don't look now, but you've officially completed the lessons in this book. How does it feel? It should feel amazing. Because taking action and figuring this stuff out — it has the potential to make you rich.

So if the lessons are over, what could possibly be next?

Further Reading

Bearing in mind the last five lessons, you might feel like your brain is full to bursting with investing know-how. You've certainly got more than enough to get started.

But if you can find a little more space in the nooks and crannies of your cranium, you can really impress your friends and even those suits at the bank.

We want to show off a list of articles that MoneyWise.com has put together to help you make decisions and *grow* as an investor — because, if you've been following along, there's a good chance you're a full-fledged investor already.

To access these articles, open a web browser and visit https://moneywise.com/hero. On the page that loads, select the corresponding bracketed number to access the article.

First, let's go back over the basics. You already know **how to invest in stocks** (1), but there will come a time when you'll need to know **how to sell stock** (2), too. You'll definitely want to know **what a stock split is** (3), so you don't run out screaming into the streets if your shares lose three-quarters of their value overnight.

And even though we've already gone over some other investing options, like those ultra-safe **savings bonds** (4), **easygoing index funds** (5) and **low-fee ETFs** (6), it's worth reading those articles to deepen your understanding. They'll help if you're trying to decide between **ETFs versus mutual funds** (7) or the various **types of mutual funds** (8) available.

You can also explore a few other possibilities we didn't cover in this book:

- Investing in "commodities" — that is, raw materials — including the **ever-popular gold** (9). Never rusts, never goes out of style.
- Checking out **Real Estate Investment Trusts** (10), or "REITS," that let you invest in real estate without buying up a whole row of homes like the Monopoly Man.
- Buying **fractions of shares** (11), so you don't need to drop hundreds of dollars on a full-size chunk of Tesla.
- **Paying off your mortgage early** (12) instead of investing, although this move only makes sense if you're extremely risk-averse.

If you're really stuck and have no idea whether you should dump your money into savings, stocks, bonds or gold, check out this eye-opening **interactive graph** (13). It shows how much money you would have today if someone invested $2,000 on your behalf through these methods when you were born.

While that graph shows just how wasteful it is to leave your cash to languish in the bank, you do need to keep at least some money at the ready in the form of **an emergency fund** (14). So be sure to familiarize yourself with the **types of bank accounts** (15) available, because some will stack up way, way more **compound interest** (16) while your money is sitting around unused. We're talking 10 or even *25 times* more interest.

It's just as important to choose the right account for your investments. If you're **investing for your kid's education** (17) or for your retirement, you gain access to a series of accounts with special tax breaks that keep Uncle Sam's grubby claws at bay.

For example, once you figure out **how much you need to save for retirement** (18), you can either go it alone through an individual retirement account — those come in **traditional IRA** (19) and spicy **Roth IRA** (20) flavors — or you can try to get your employer to help out through a **pension** (21) or **401(k)** (22).

And that's it! At least, that's it for this book.

Investing is a bottomless pit, if you want it to be; even a billionaire like Warren Buffett reads five newspapers every day to stay informed on new opportunities.

If you care more about *keeping up* than *getting ahead*, you're already good to go; otherwise, keep checking MoneyWise.com for more guides, reviews and news to help you succeed.

And be sure to share this book with your friends, family and anyone else you think is ready to go from zero to hero.

Happy investing!

CPSIA information can be obtained
at www.ICGtesting.com
Printed in the USA
LVHW070553300921
699027LV00007B/71

9 781649 699633